But it's my turn to leave you . . .

Mel Calman

But it's my turn
to leave you...

Methuen

First published in 1980 by
Eyre Methuen Ltd
Reprinted 1980 (twice), 1981 (twice)
Reprinted 1983 and 1987 by
Methuen London Ltd
11 New Fetter Lane, London EC4P 4EE

Copyright © Mel Calman 1980
Designed by Philip Thompson

ISBN 0 413 47580 8

Printed in Great Britain
by Richard Clay Ltd, Bungay, Suffolk

To my ex-wives . . . for their help with the research . . .

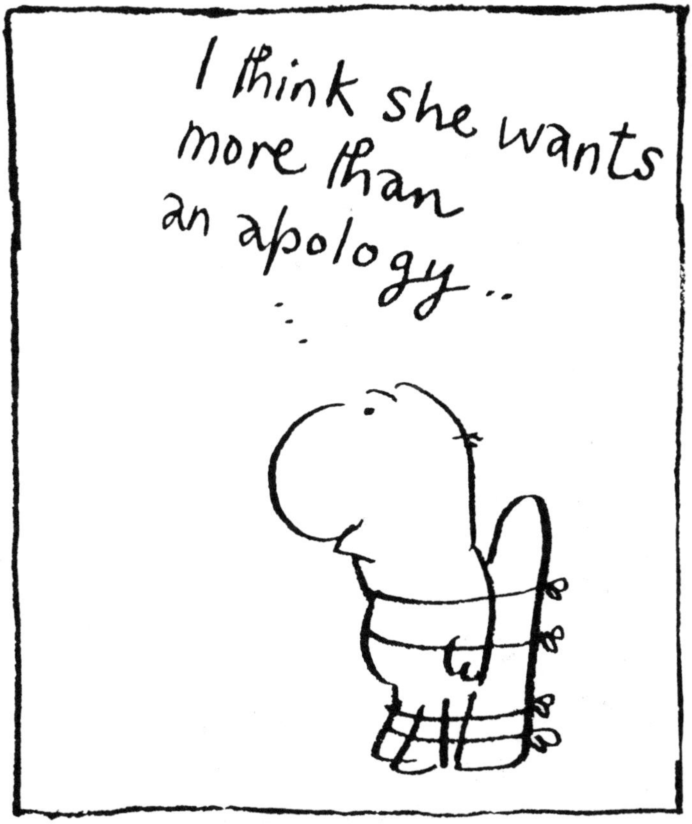
I think she wants more than an apology...

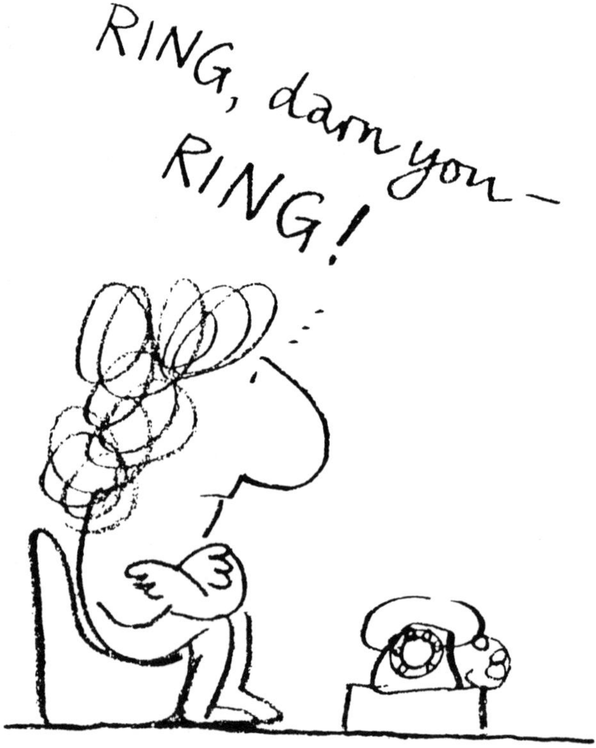
RING, darn you-
RING!

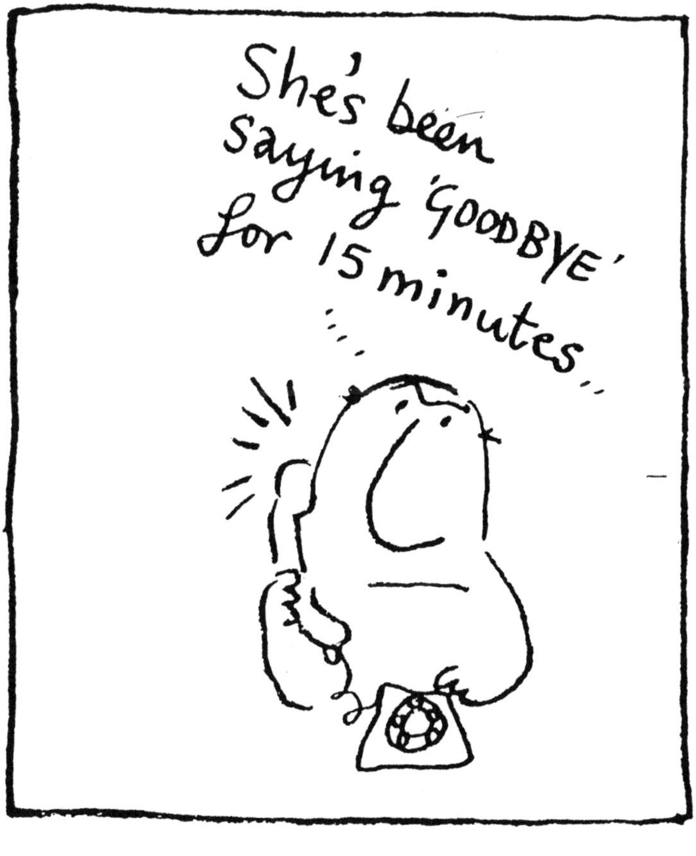
She's been saying 'GOODBYE' for 15 minutes...

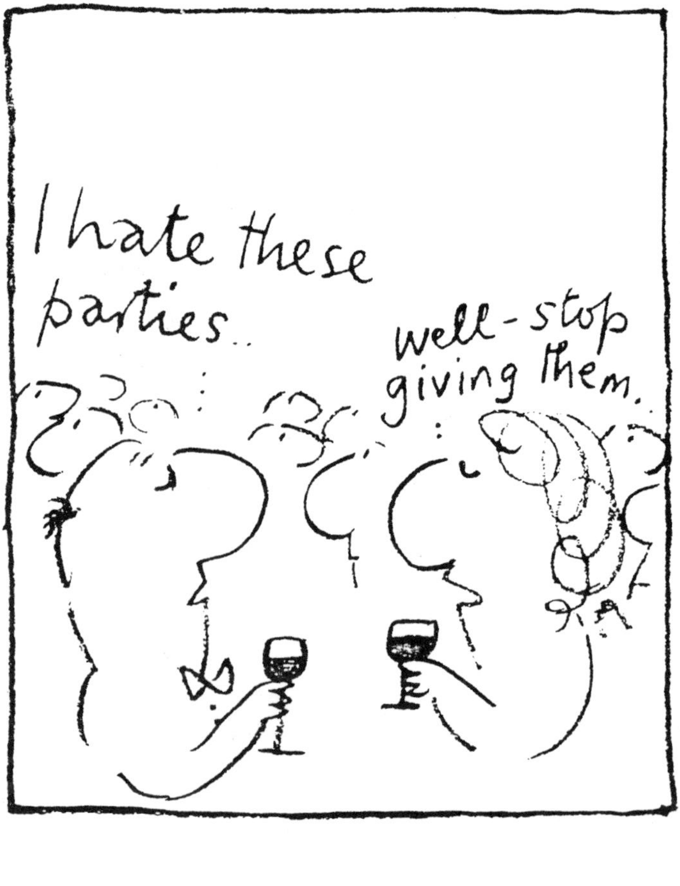
I hate these parties..
well-stop giving them..

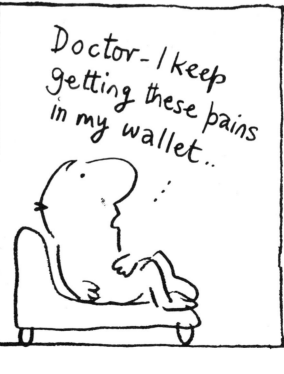

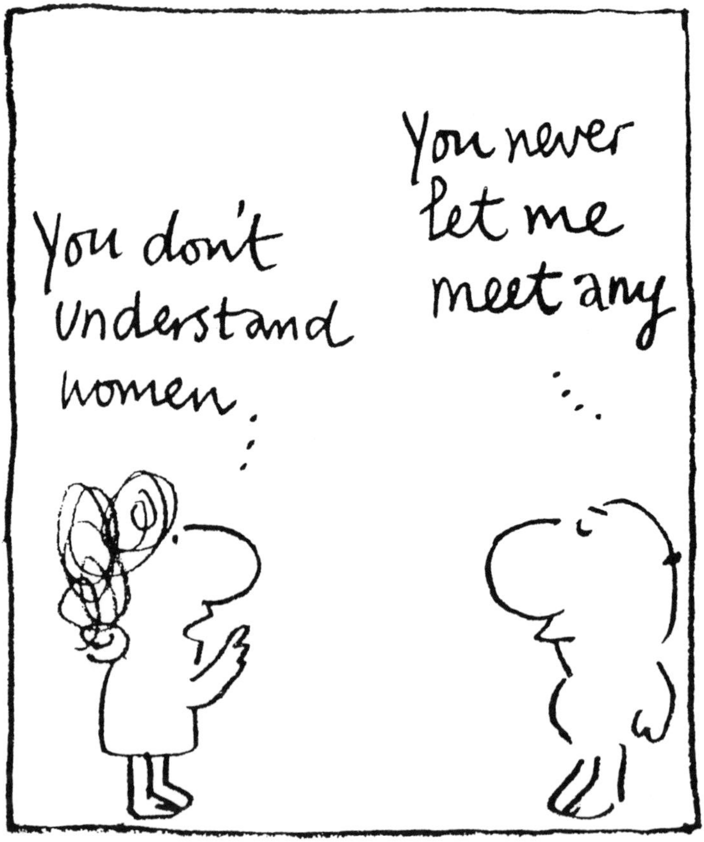
You don't understand women
You never let me meet any

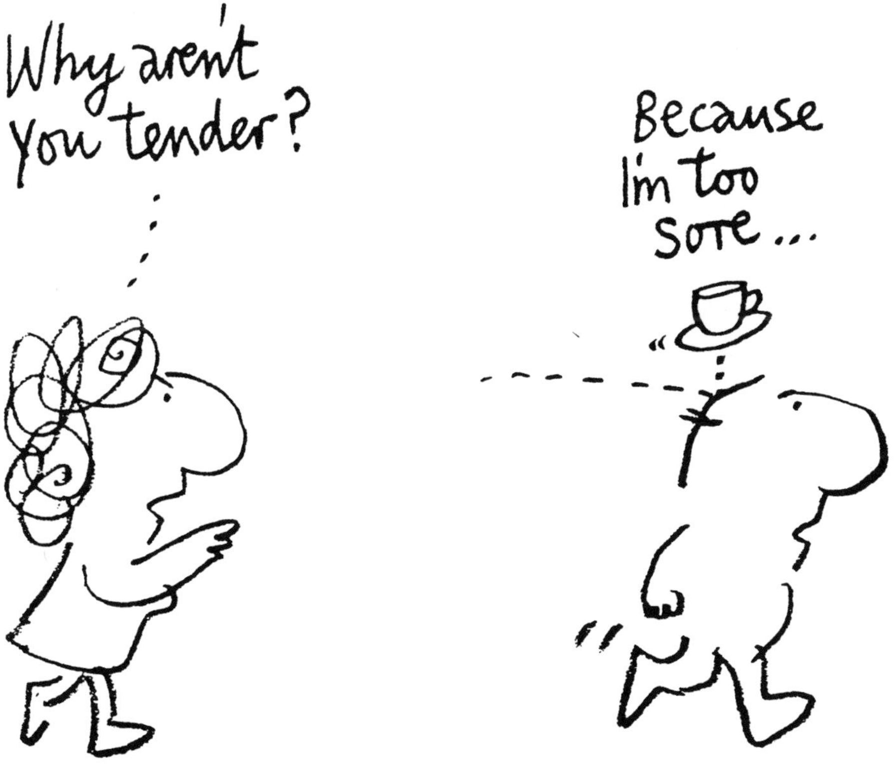
Why aren't you tender?
Because I'm too sore...

The trouble with marriage is that it has deprived me of adult conversation
ZZZ

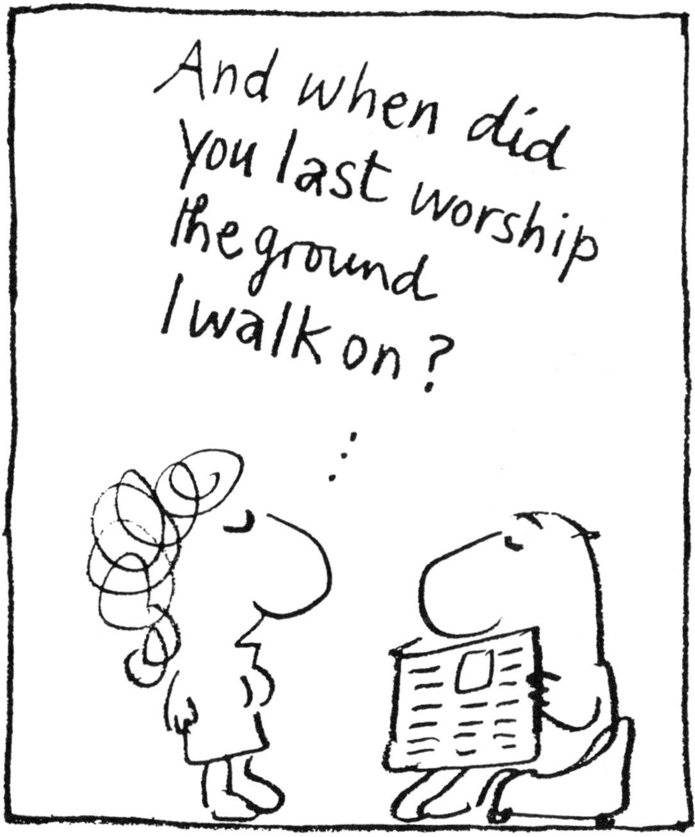
And when did you last worship the ground I walk on?
. . .

And don't talk to me
until you're ready
to listen!

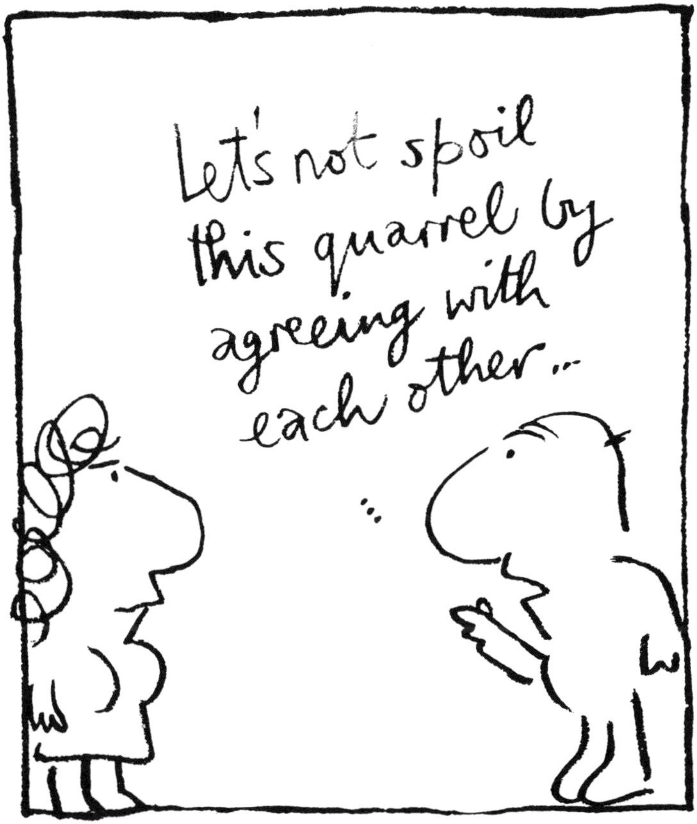
Let's not spoil this quarrel by agreeing with each other...
...

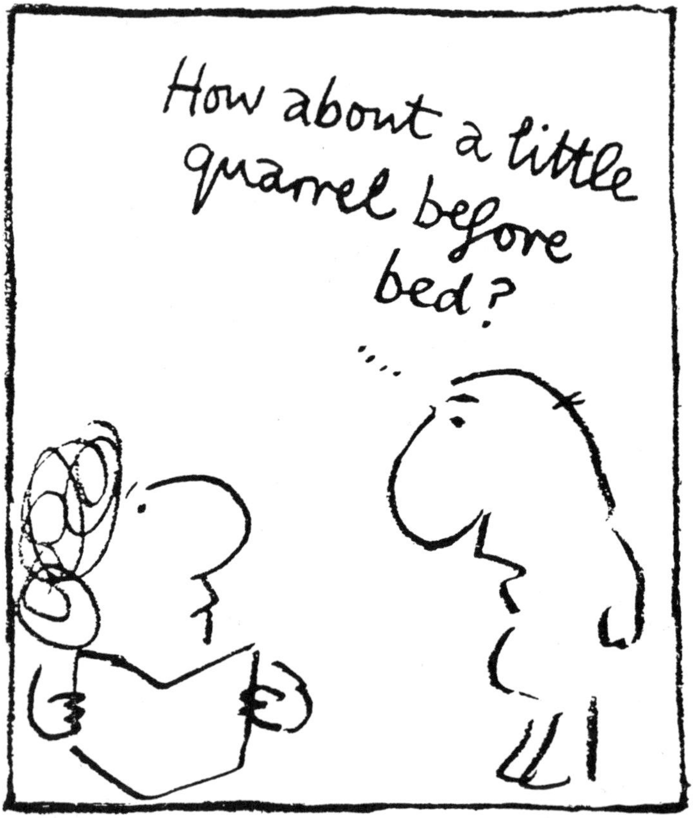
How about a little quarrel before bed?

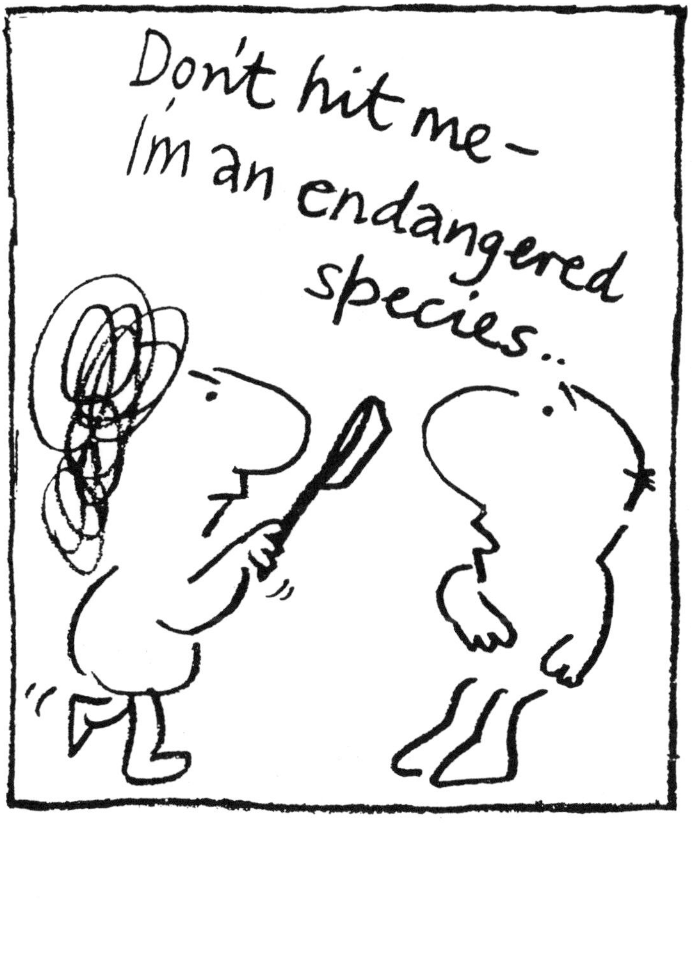
Don't hit me -
I'm an endangered
species..

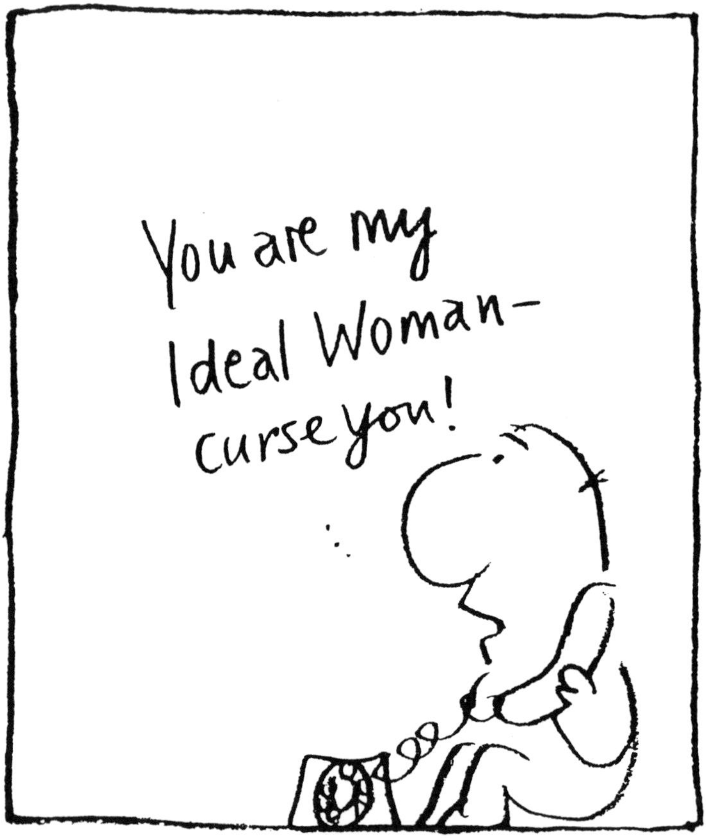
You are my
Ideal Woman-
curse you!

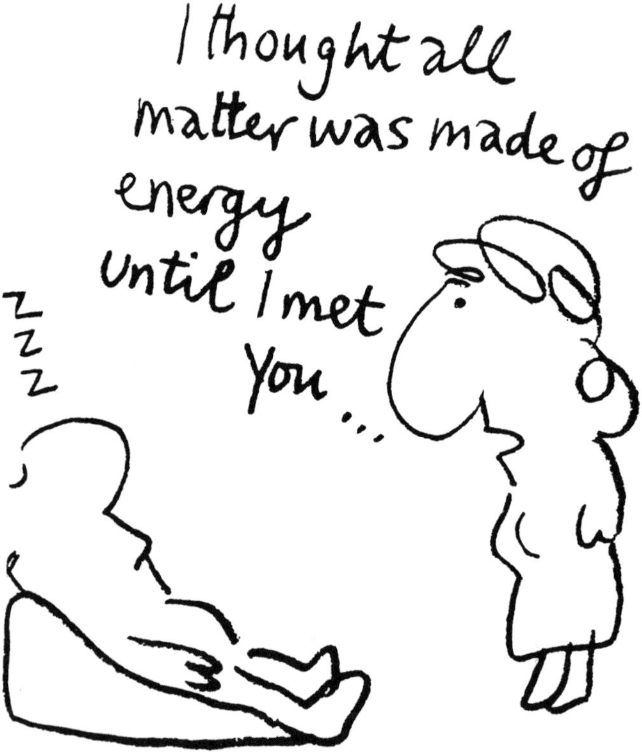
I thought all matter was made of energy until I met you...
ZZZ

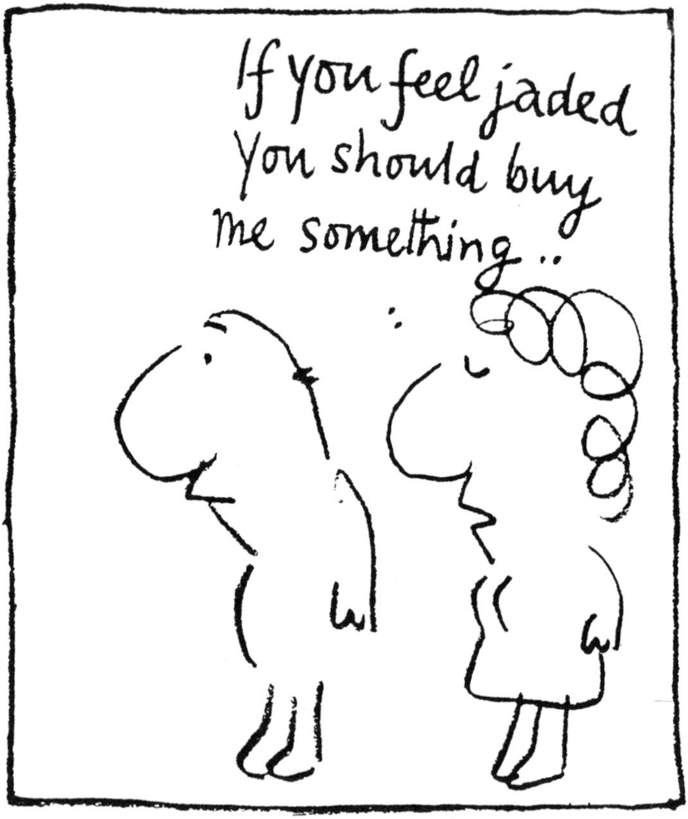
If you feel jaded
you should buy
me something..

I suppose a shallow person might find it profound...
Noël Coward told me he hated people who name-dropped..
That's just a female attitude..

Here's to Temperance..
I remember you - You came up, to me at last years party and asked me if I remembered you..
Step outside and say that!
Now tell me all about yourself - briefly...

We've nothing against women - we just don't lend them money...
LOANS

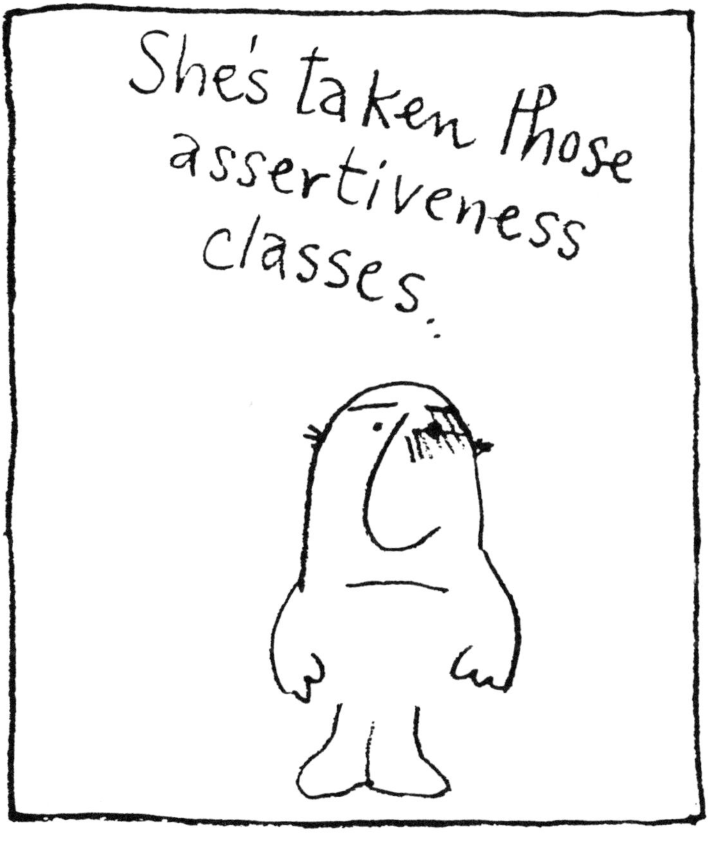
She's taken those
assertiveness
classes..

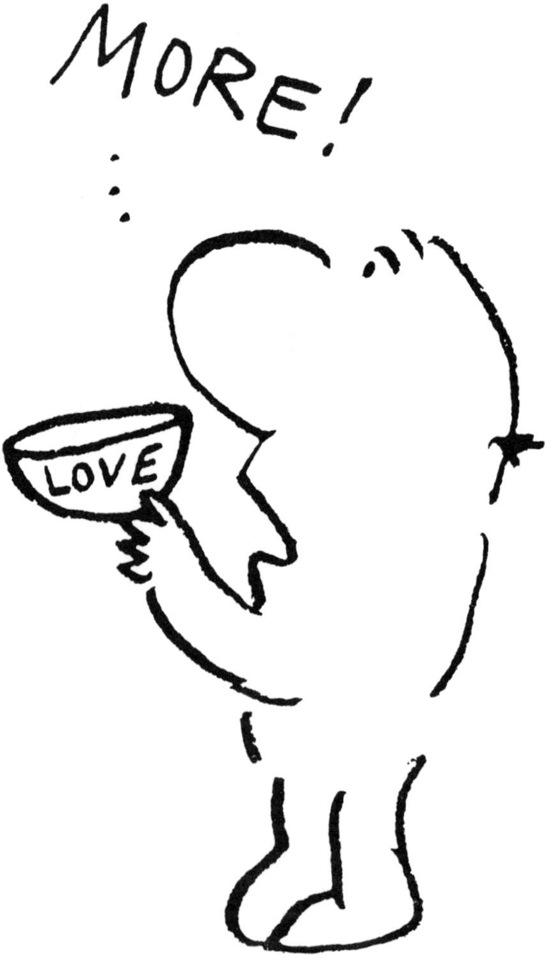
MORE!
LOVE

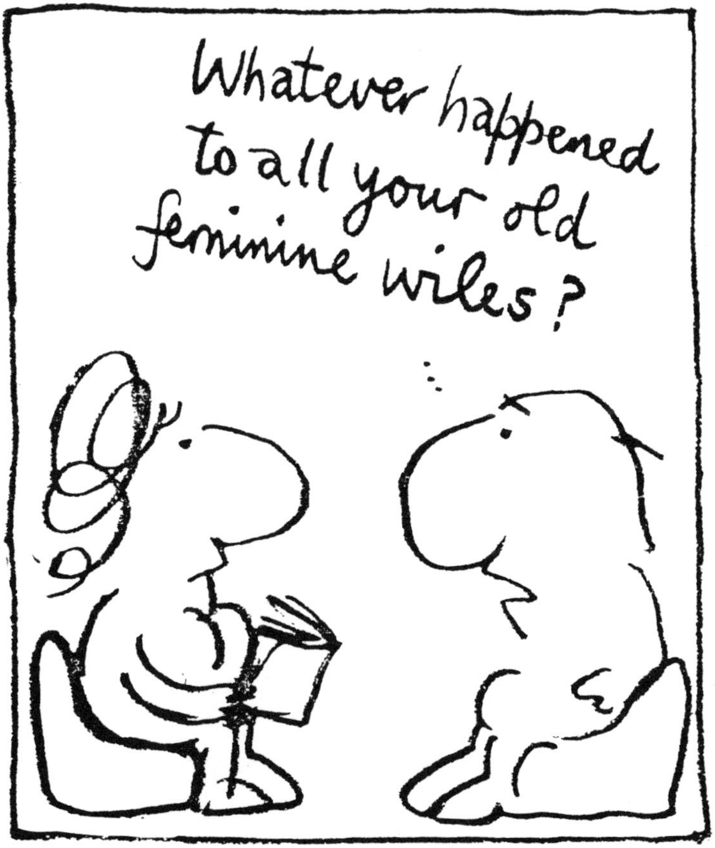
Whatever happened to all your old feminine wiles?

What makes me cross is you always saying I'm cross...

It's only you that's incompatible...

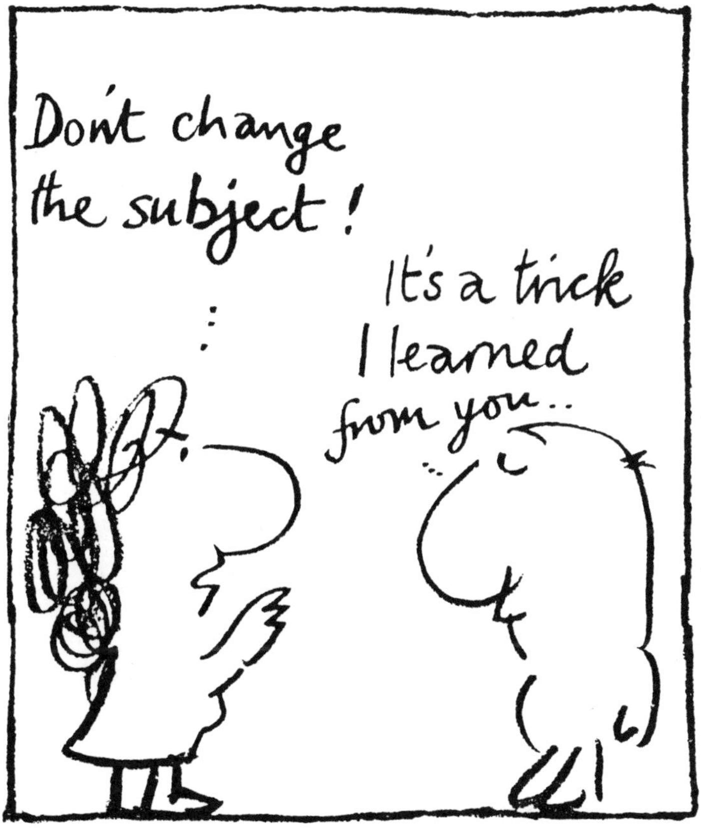
Don't change the subject!
It's a trick I learned from you...

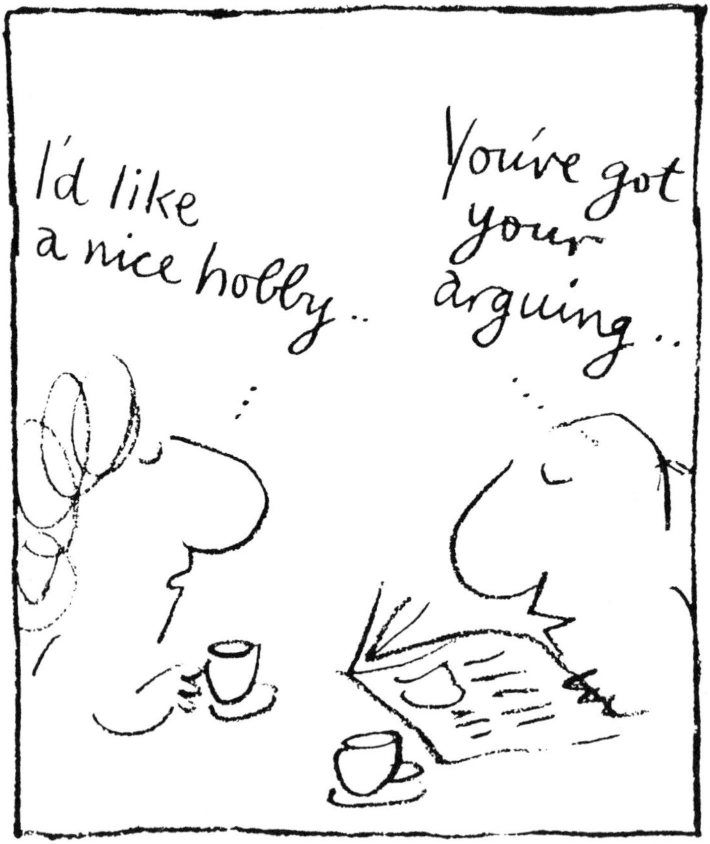
I'd like a nice hobby..
You've got your arguing..

Look at it
from my
point of
view...

You're too
far away

Whose side are you on– mine or his?
MINE - of course
Don't confuse me with facts
A real man doesn't want the last word..
Yes, dear!
Did you say I wasn't GENTLE?

Something's missing from this romantic dinner...

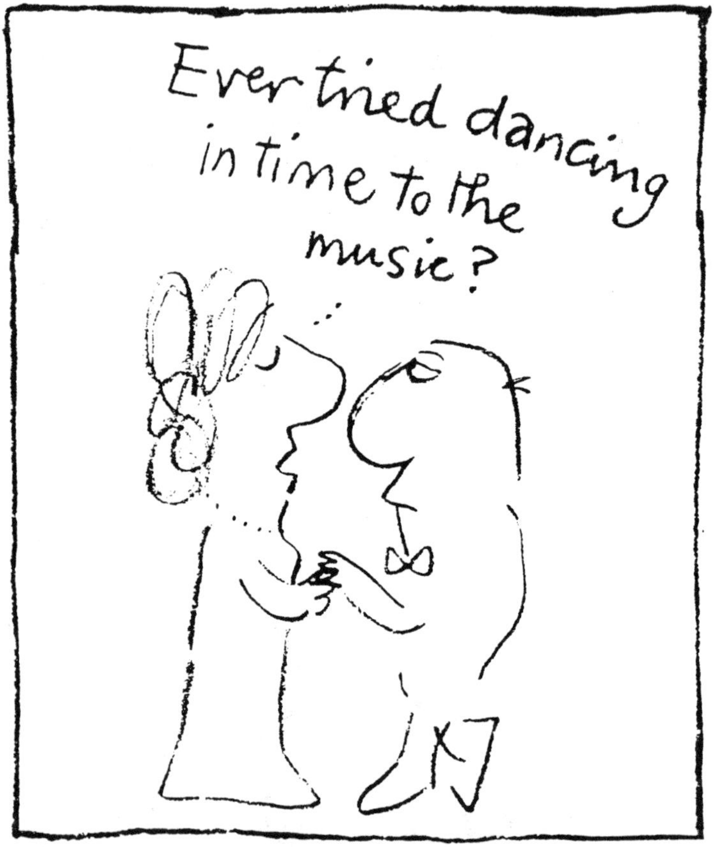
Ever tried dancing in time to the music?

Some awful man pressed his knee against mine all evening
That was me..

I need this space between us - so as to be close to you...

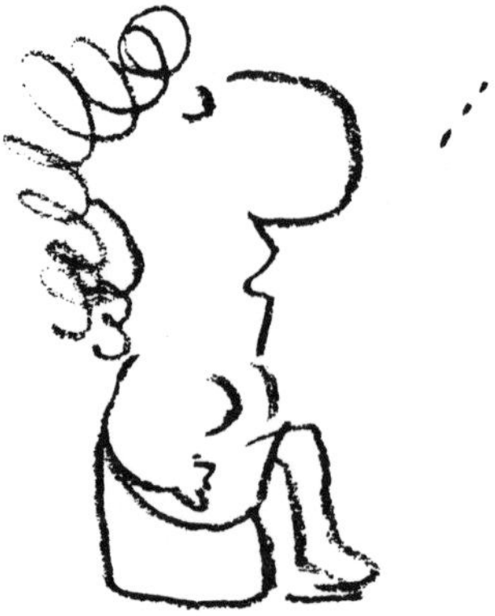

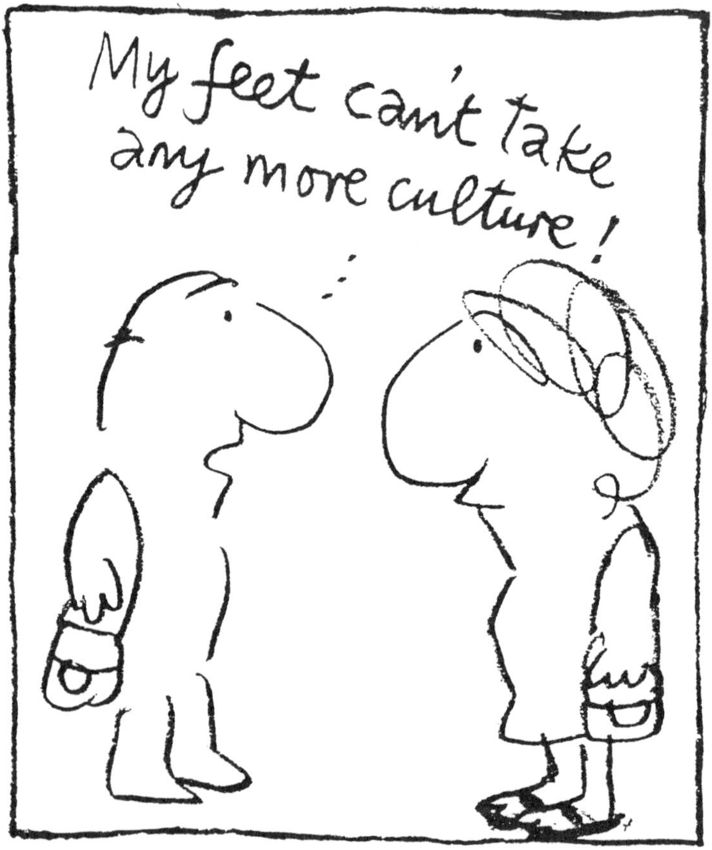
My feet can't take any more culture!

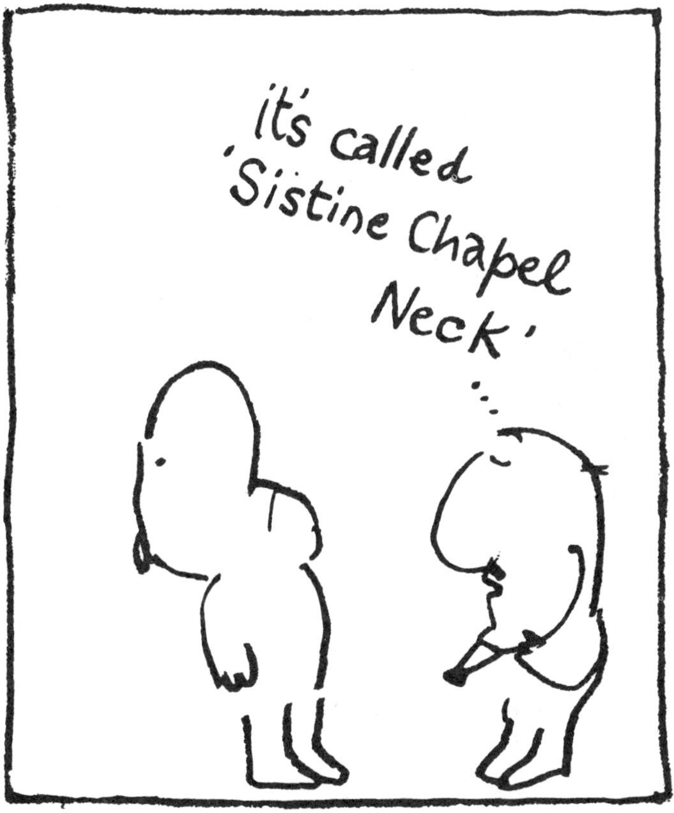
it's called 'Sistine Chapel Neck'

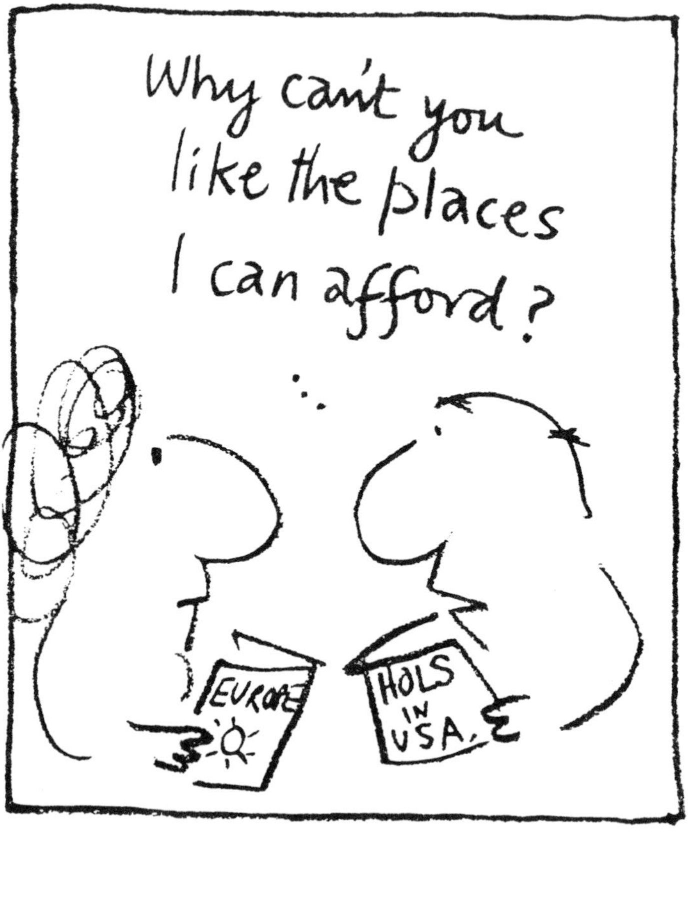
Why can't you like the places I can afford?
EUROPE
HOLS IN USA.

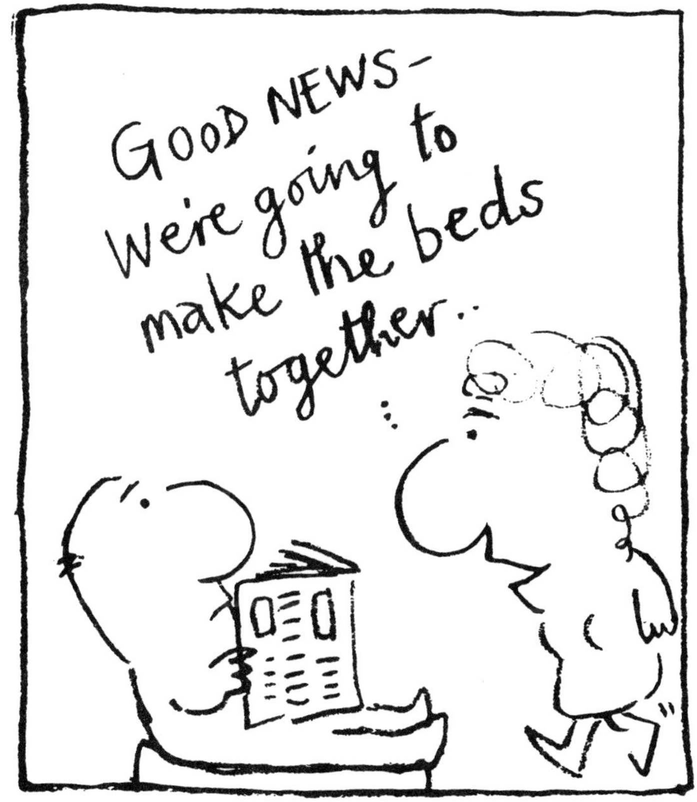
GOOD NEWS-
We're going to
make the beds
together..

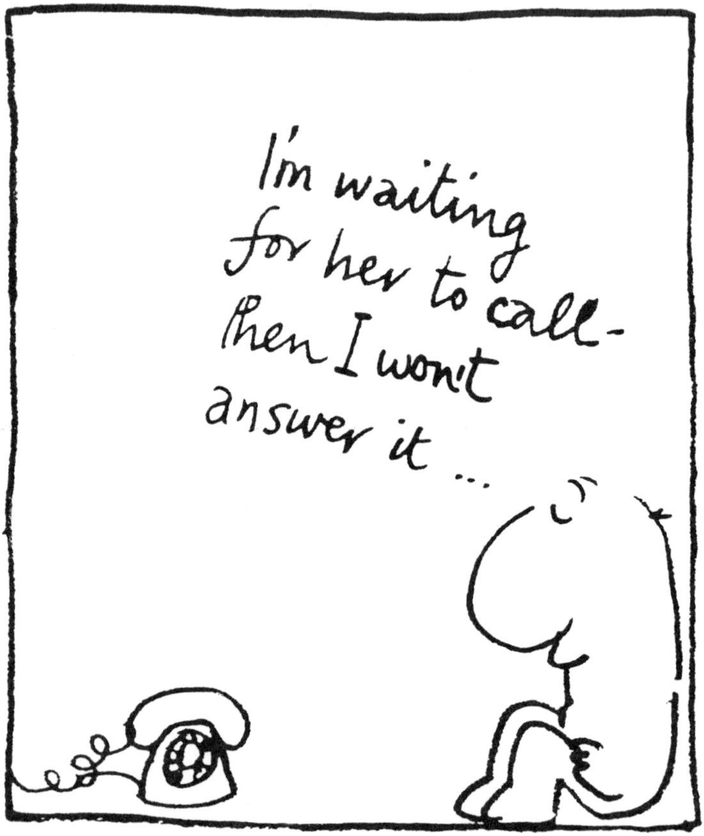
I'm waiting for her to call- then I won't answer it ...

The only person
who writes to me
is the subscription
girl at
"TIME" ...
magazine

I tried an Encounter
Group – but
I didn't meet anyone...

It must be
the mirror
that's ill ..

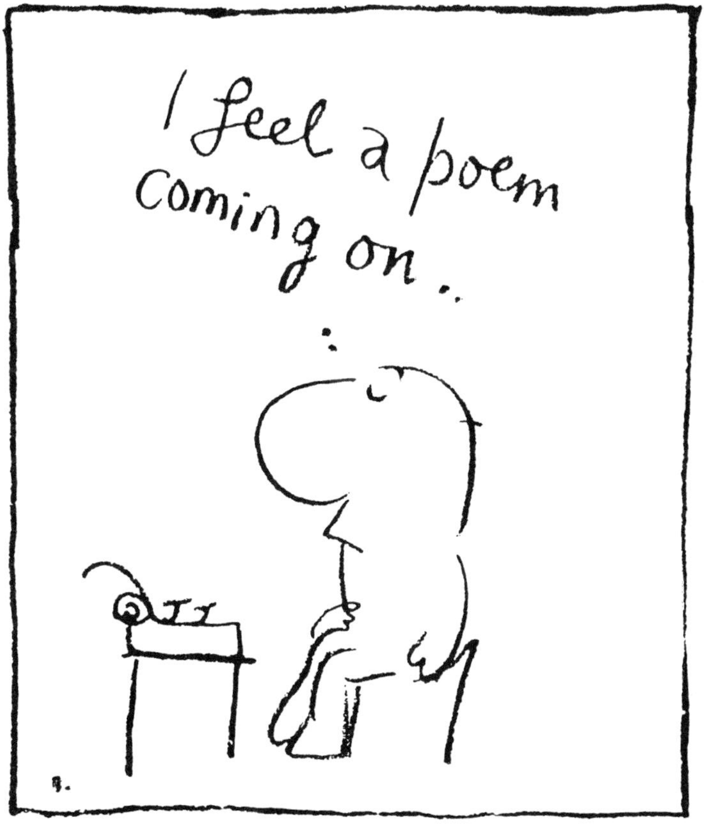
I feel a poem coming on ..

Jogging is like
marriage - tiring
but good for you...

Food is a
four-letter
word here...

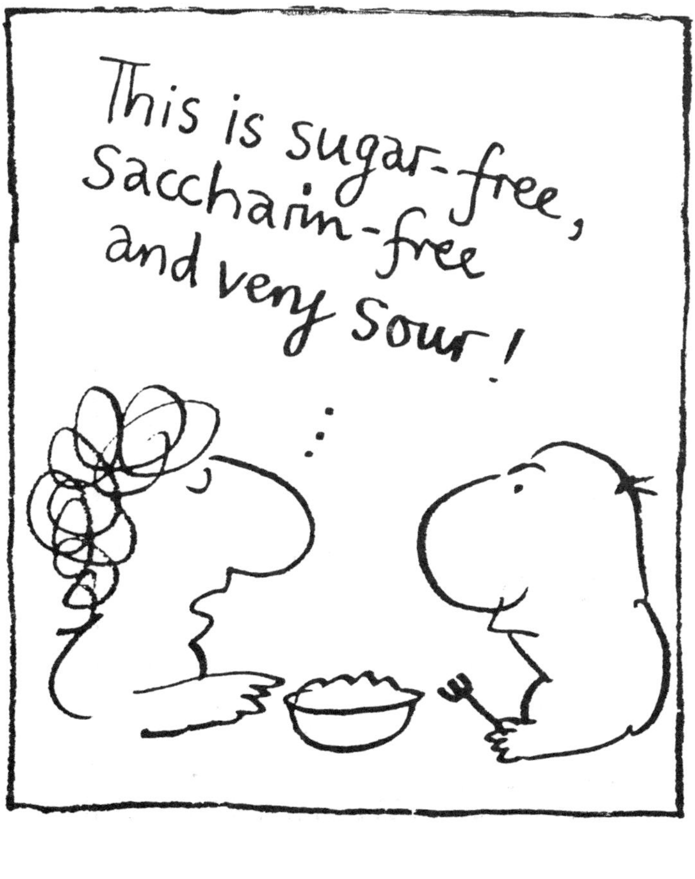
This is sugar-free, saccharin-free and very sour!

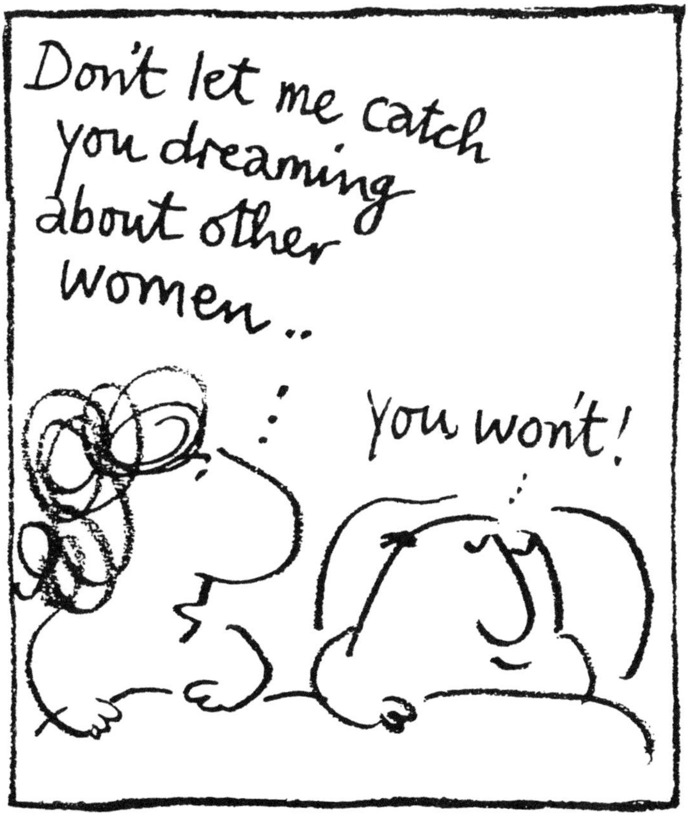
Don't let me catch you dreaming about other women..
You won't!

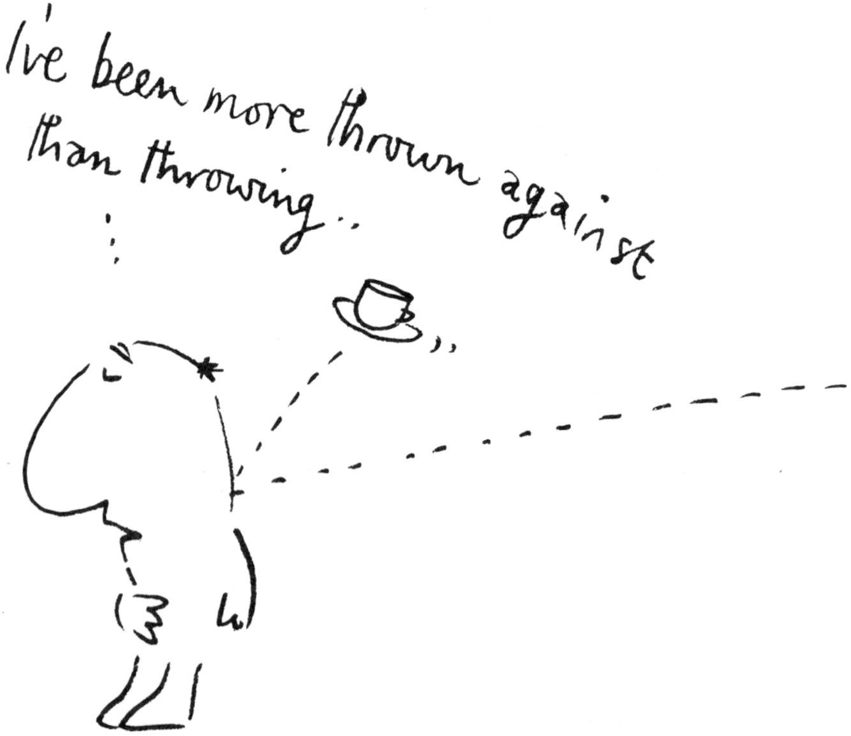
I've been more thrown against than throwing..

CULTURE–HAH! You're only interested in foreign women!
...
FRANCE IS FUN!

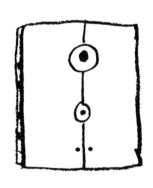

I understand it
and I still don't
like it

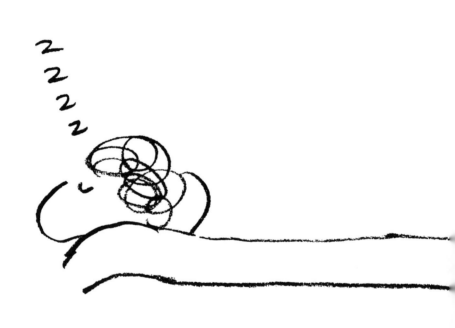

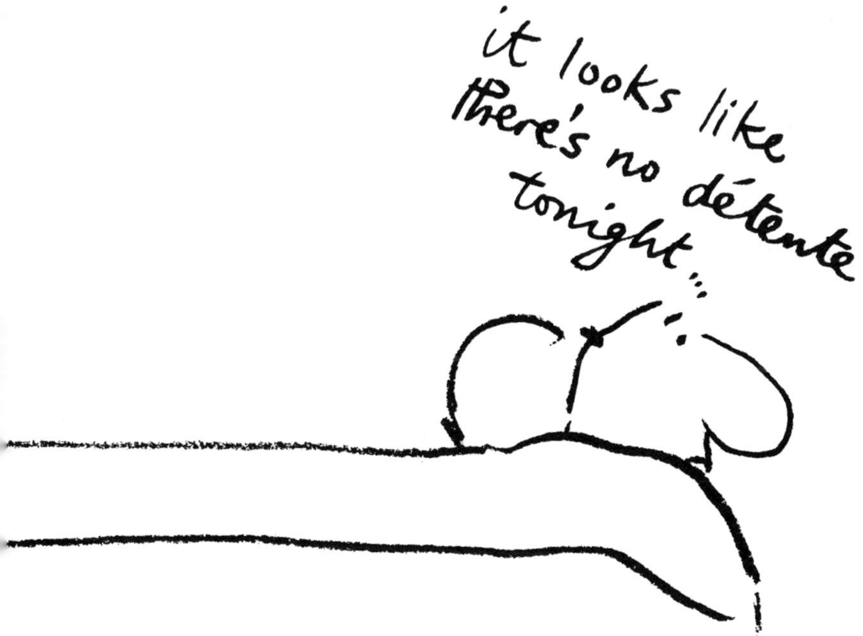
it looks like
there's no détente
tonight...

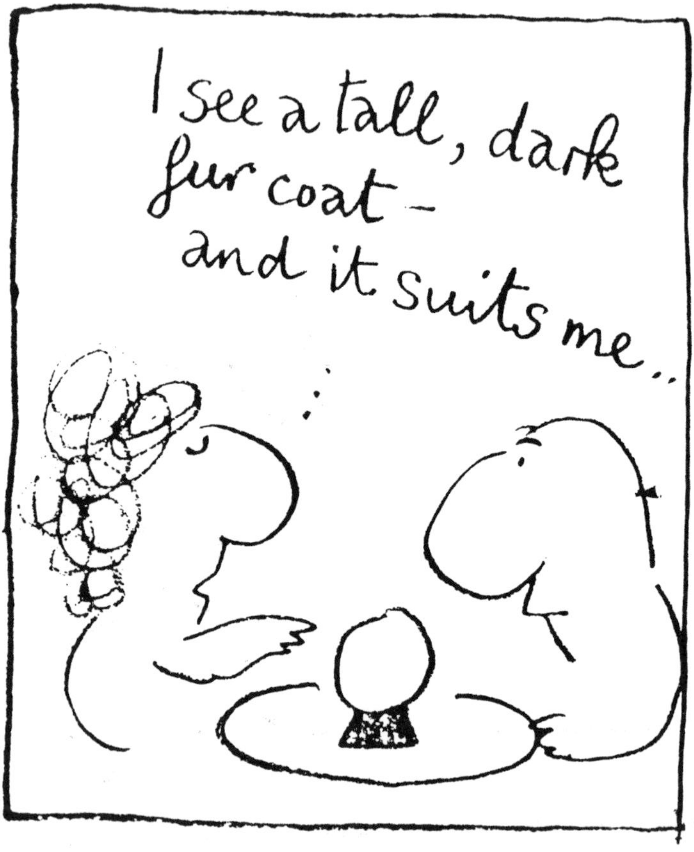
I see a tall, dark fur coat - and it suits me...

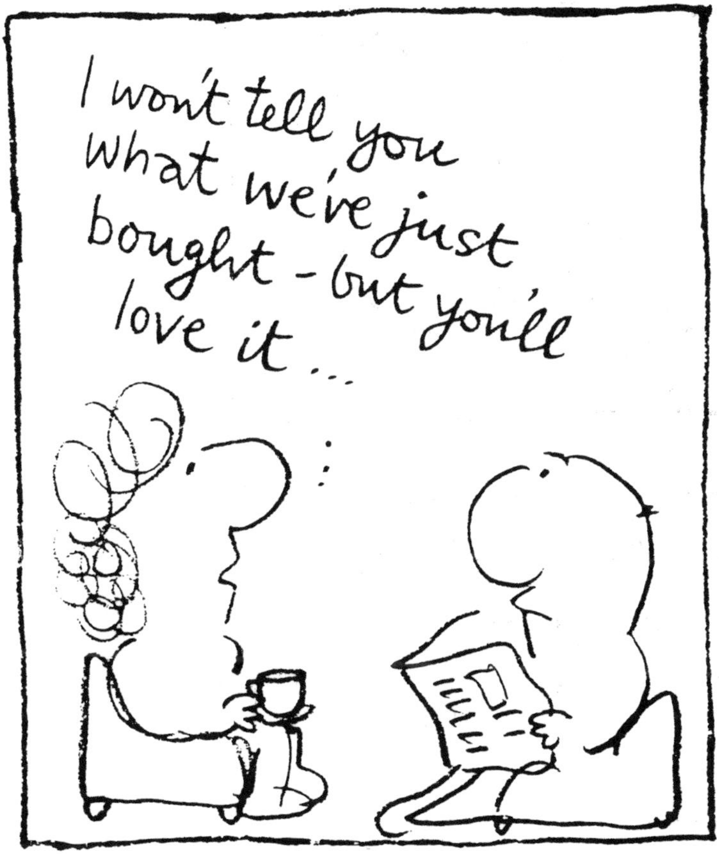
I won't tell you what we've just bought - but you'll love it ...

At least she still
sends me
her bills...

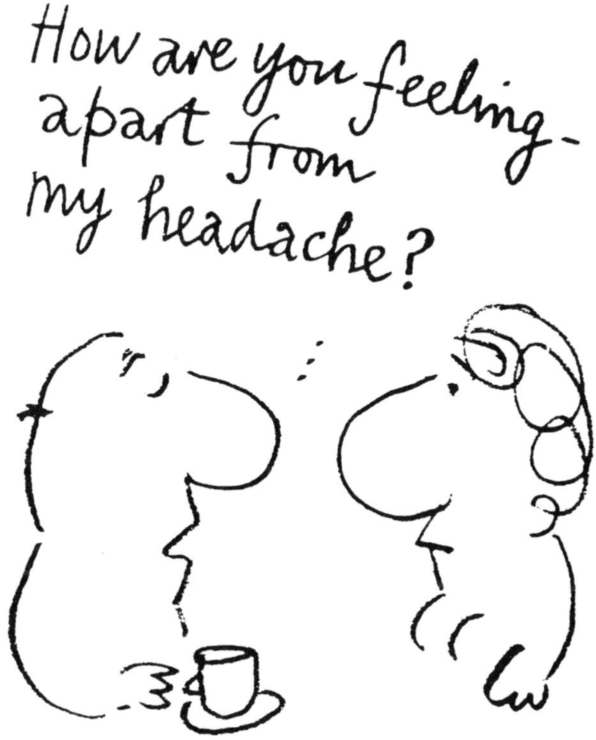
How are you feeling -
apart from
my headache?

You can't put me on a pedestal and then expect me ... to dust it ..

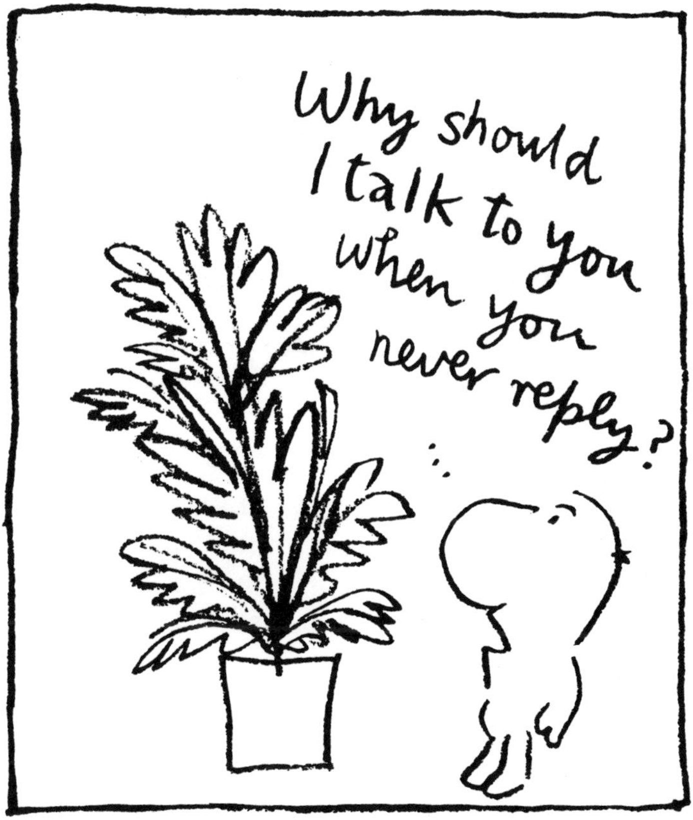
Why should I talk to you when you never reply?

You're the kind of man who takes his clothes off and is wearing another suit underneath

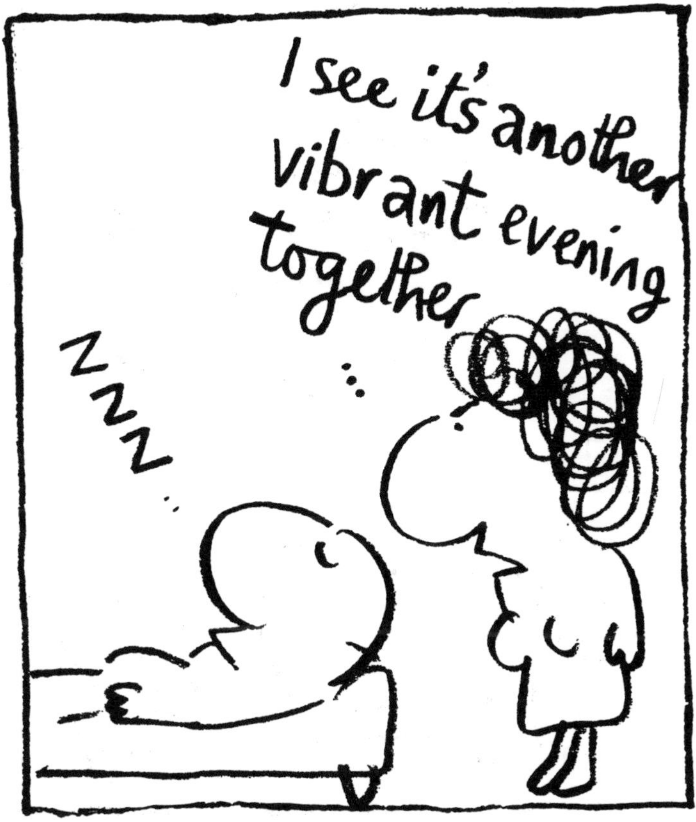
I see it's another vibrant evening together
...
ZZZ ..

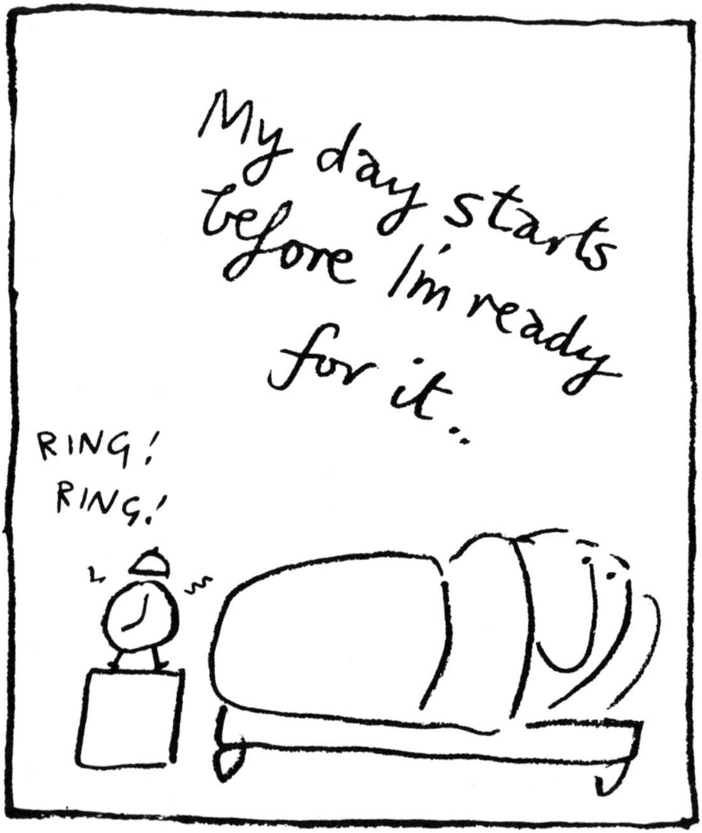
My day starts before I'm ready for it..
RING!
RING!

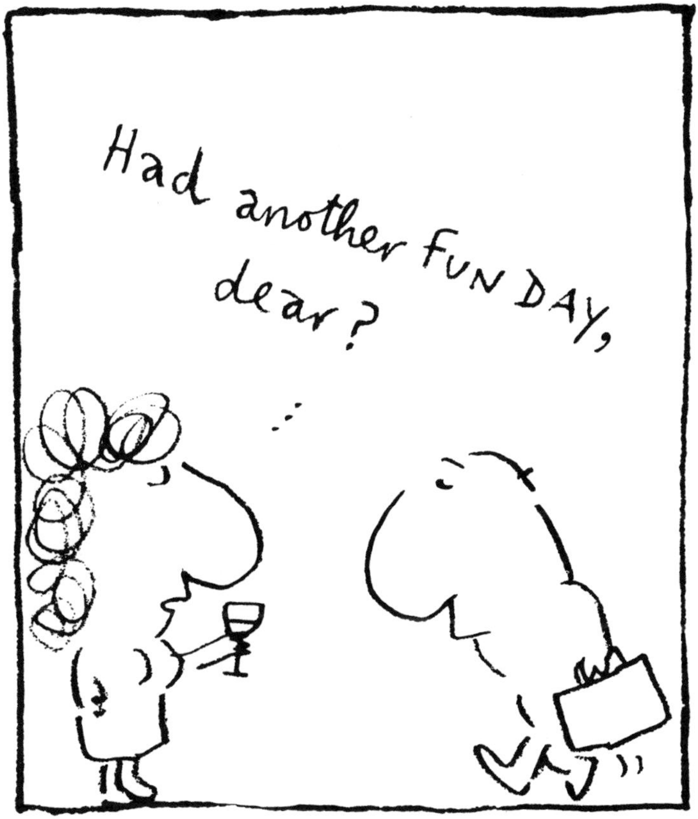
Had another FUN DAY, dear?
. . .

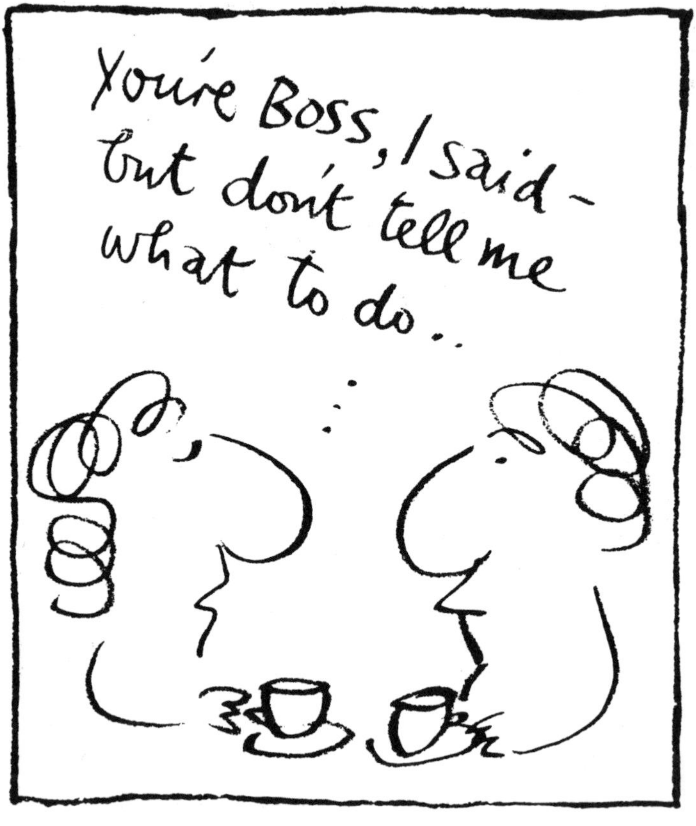
You're Boss, I said -
but don't tell me
what to do . . .

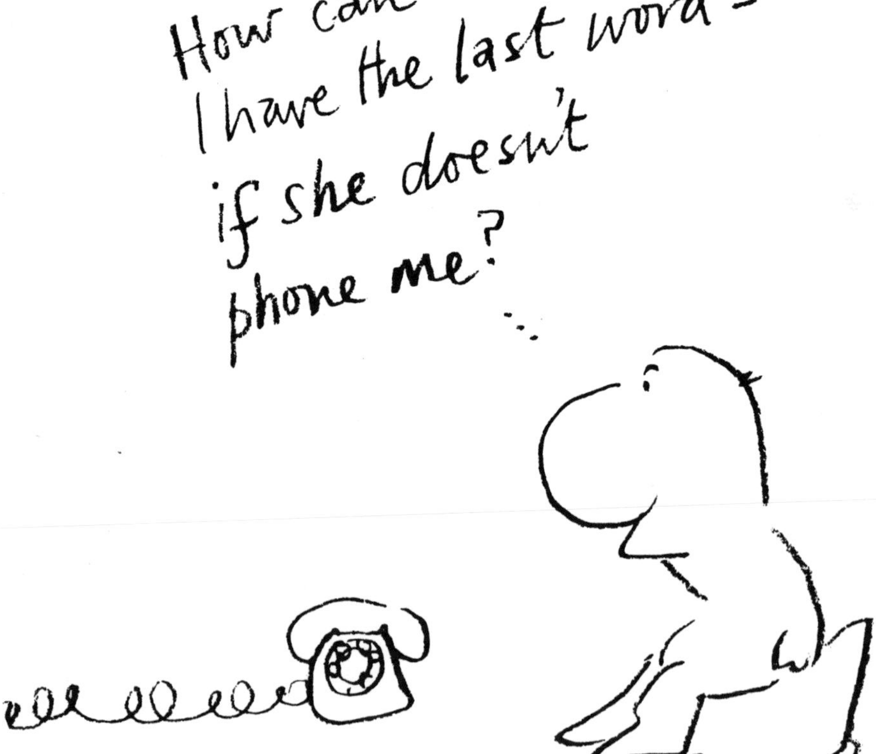
How can
I have the last word -
if she doesn't
phone me?